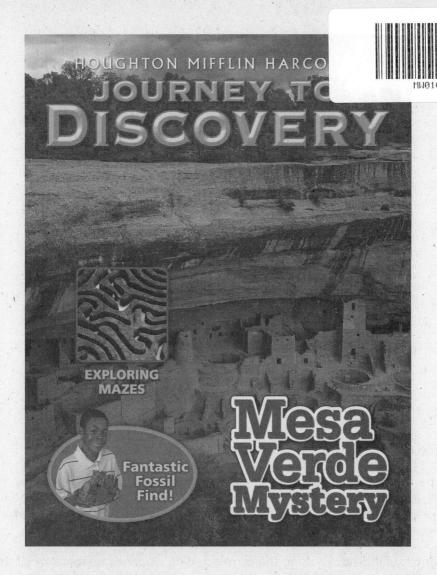

HOUGHTON MIFFLIN HARCOURT

JOURNEY TO DISCOVERY

EXPLORING MAZES

Fantastic Fossil Find!

Mesa Verde Mystery

Novel Unit Assessments

- Weekly Tests
- Novel Comprehension Tests
- Fluency Test

GRADE

5

HOUGHTON MIFFLIN HARCOURT

TEST RECORD FORM	Possible Score	Criterion Score	Student Score
A: **Vocabulary** Multiple-Meaning Words	10	8	
B: **Comprehension** Text and Graphic Features	5	4	
C: **Phonics** Prefixes and Word Roots	10	8	
D: **Language Arts** Possessive Nouns	10	8	
TOTAL	35	28	
Total Student Score x 2.85 =			%

Multiple-Meaning Words

Identify the definition that applies to the underlined word.

Vocabulary Dictionary

smart (smärt) v. **1.** to feel a sharp stinging pain **2.** to cause such a sharp stinging pain **3.** to feel shame or remorse

adj. **1.** having or showing quick intelligence **2.** impressively neat or trim in appearance, as in dress **3.** clever, witty

---

1. Chloe's outfit is very <u>smart</u> today.

○ **A.** *v.* definition 1

○ **B.** *v.* definition 2

○ **C.** *adj.* definition 1

○ **D.** *adj.* definition 2

2. Carlos always makes me laugh with his <u>smart</u> comments.

○ **A.** *v.* definition 3

○ **B.** *adj.* definition 1

○ **C.** *adj.* definition 2

○ **D.** *adj.* definition 3

3. My eldest brother is the <u>smartest</u> in our family.

○ **A.** *v.* definition 3

○ **B.** *adj.* definition 1

○ **C.** *adj.* definition 2

○ **D.** *adj.* definition 3

4. This bruise on my knee is <u>smarting</u>.

○ **A.** *v.* definition 1

○ **B.** *v.* definition 3

○ **C.** *adj.* definition 1

○ **D.** *adj.* definition 3

GO ON ➡

Vocabulary Multiple-Meaning Words

5. The lecture I received from Ms. O'Donnel <u>smarted</u>.

- ○ **A.** *v.* definition 1
- ◉ **B.** *v.* definition 3
- ○ **C.** *adj.* definition 1
- ○ **D.** *adj.* definition 2

Select the choice that best replaces the underlined word.

6. Mimi <u>struggled</u> to lift the heavy box.

- ○ **A.** battled
- ○ **B.** labored
- ○ **C.** suffered
- ○ **D.** worried

7. The computer game was <u>flawed</u> due to an error in the program.

- ○ **A.** damaged
- ○ **B.** incomplete
- ○ **C.** perfect
- ○ **D.** unbroken

8. The runner began slowly and <u>gradually</u> increased her speed.

- ○ **A.** little by little
- ○ **B.** inch by inch
- ○ **C.** drop by drop
- ○ **D.** piece by piece

9. Once Yuri learned the basic steps, he could perform the <u>routine</u> well.

- ○ **A.** character
- ○ **B.** curtain
- ○ **C.** dance
- ○ **D.** gag

10. Reina painted the fence with long, <u>sweeping</u> strokes of the paintbrush.

- ○ **A.** broad
- ○ **B.** cleaning
- ○ **C.** powerful
- ○ **D.** total

Text and Graphic Features

Identify the choice that best completes the statement or answers the question.

1. The photos and captions in this passage
   - ○ **A.** show how animals use their senses.
   - ○ **B.** are not needed to understand the article.
   - ○ **C.** help the reader understand animal navigation.
   - ○ **D.** simply show the kinds of animals discussed in the article.

2. What does the photograph on page 6 indicate?
   - ○ **A.** that Pacific salmon return home
   - ○ **B.** that salmon use the sun and stars to navigate
   - ○ **C.** that salmon begin their lives in the Pacific Ocean
   - ○ **D.** that salmon swim out in the ocean and never return

3. Under which subheading can the reader learn about infrasound?
   - ○ **A.** Leaving Home
   - ○ **B.** Elephant Talk
   - ○ **C.** Why Bees Sing and Dance
   - ○ **D.** Bird Maps and Compasses

4. Which text feature helps you understand how echolocation works?
   - ○ **A.** the caption on page 8
   - ○ **B.** the subheading on page 8
   - ○ **C.** the arrow on page 9
   - ○ **D.** the photo of the bat

5. From the photo on page 11, the reader can tell that

○ **A.** whooping cranes do not migrate.

○ **B.** whooping cranes always follow airplanes.

○ **C.** some birds are guided by their own compasses.

○ **D.** some birds need people to help them migrate.

Mark Student Reading Level:

_____ Independent _____ Instructional _____ Listening

Prefixes and Word Roots

Identify the correctly spelled choice to complete the sentence.

1. My class took a trip to the wildlife _____.

   ○ **A.** perserve
   ○ **B.** preserv
   ○ **C.** preserve
   ○ **D.** proserve

2. The ranger expressed _____ about endangered animals living in the park.

   ○ **A.** comcern
   ○ **B.** concern
   ○ **C.** consern
   ○ **D.** cuncern

3. She said that the park must _____ certain rules for visitors.

   ○ **A.** enforce
   ○ **B.** enforse
   ○ **C.** inforce
   ○ **D.** inforse

4. She explained that the rules help maintain the good _____ of the park.

   ○ **A.** condishun
   ○ **B.** condision
   ○ **C.** condition
   ○ **D.** cundition

GO ON →

5. We can _____ more ideas about wildlife next week.

- ○ **A.** exchainge
- ○ **B.** exchang
- ○ **C.** exchange
- ○ **D.** xchange

6. I wanted her to _____ teaching us today.

- ○ **A.** comtinue
- ○ **B.** conmtinew
- ○ **C.** continew
- ○ **D.** continue

7. I started to _____ as we got back on the bus.

- ○ **A.** pertest
- ○ **B.** portest
- ○ **C.** pretest
- ○ **D.** protest

8. My father received a _____ at work.

- ○ **A.** permotion
- ○ **B.** premotion
- ○ **C.** promotion
- ○ **D.** promotoin

9. There was a _____ among the salespeople.

- ○ **A.** comtest
- ○ **B.** contest
- ○ **C.** countest
- ○ **D.** contist

10. The _____ was to see who could sell the most.

- ○ **A.** porpoise
- ○ **B.** preporse
- ○ **C.** purpoise
- ○ **D.** purpose

Assessment Tip: Total 10 points

Possessive Nouns

Identify the choice that best completes the statement.

1. The _____ club was having a party.

  ○ **A.** woman's
  ○ **B.** womans'
  ○ **C.** women's
  ○ **D.** womens'

2. I love to shop in the _____ department.

  ○ **A.** child's
  ○ **B.** children's
  ○ **C.** childrens
  ○ **D.** childrens'

3. The head _____ goal is to get the team to work together.

  ○ **A.** coach
  ○ **B.** coach's
  ○ **C.** coache's
  ○ **D.** coaches

4. The _____ top skier is coming to speak to us.

  ○ **A.** countrie's
  ○ **B.** countries
  ○ **C.** country's
  ○ **D.** countrys'

5. The _____ division race will begin tomorrow morning.

  ○ **A.** man's
  ○ **B.** mans'
  ○ **C.** men's
  ○ **D.** mens'

6. Our _____ volunteers have done a better job than the volunteers from any other city.

   ○ **A.** citie's
   ○ **B.** cities
   ○ **C.** citys'
   ○ **D.** city's

7. _____ expectations for the team are very high.

   ○ **A.** People's
   ○ **B.** Peoples'
   ○ **C.** Peoples
   ○ **D.** Persons'

8. The runners from this community will help raise money for the _____ children.

   ○ **A.** communitie's
   ○ **B.** communities
   ○ **C.** community's
   ○ **D.** communitys'

9. Lacrosse is new to this town, but the _____ appeal is growing every year.

   ○ **A.** sport's
   ○ **B.** sporte's
   ○ **C.** sports
   ○ **D.** sports'

10. One little _____ balloon went floating up into the clouds.

   ○ **A.** boy
   ○ **B.** boy's
   ○ **C.** boys
   ○ **D.** boys'

Name _____ Date _____

TEST RECORD FORM	Possible Score	Criterion Score	Student Score
A: **Vocabulary** Suffixes *-ness, -less, -ment*	10	8	
B: **Comprehension** Understanding Characters	5	4	
C: **Decoding** Suffixes	10	8	
D: **Language Arts** Titles and Abbreviations	10	8	
TOTAL	35	28	
Total Student Score x 2.85 =			%

GO ON

Suffixes *-ness*, *-less*, *-ment*

Identify the choice that best defines the underlined word.

1. The <u>happiness</u> she felt showed on her face.

   ○ **A.** wanting to be happy
   ○ **B.** the power to be happy
   ○ **C.** not wanting to be happy
   ○ **D.** the condition of being happy

2. In her <u>excitement</u> she did not see the edge of the stage.

   ○ **A.** not being excited
   ○ **B.** able to be excited
   ○ **C.** wanting to be excited
   ○ **D.** the condition of being excited

3. His <u>ruthlessness</u> was hurting everyone.

   ○ **A.** lack of Ruth
   ○ **B.** lack of rottenness
   ○ **C.** lack of compassion
   ○ **D.** abundance of compassion

4. The boy was <u>speechless</u> after he received his award.

   ○ **A.** using speech
   ○ **B.** full of speech
   ○ **C.** without speech
   ○ **D.** able to have speech

5. The man was <u>penniless</u>.

   ○ **A.** without money
   ○ **B.** had too much money
   ○ **C.** a collector of pennies
   ○ **D.** a beggar who took pennies

GO ON

Vocabulary Suffixes -*ness*,
-*less*, -*ment*

6. The soccer team raised a <u>tremendous</u> amount of money to
pay for their uniforms.

○ **A.** fabulous
○ **B.** great
○ **C.** small
○ **D.** terrible

7. Edith enjoyed vacationing in <u>remote</u> island villages.

○ **A.** faraway
○ **B.** foreign
○ **C.** nearby
○ **D.** unknown

8. The planet Mars has a dusty, rocky, and hilly <u>terrain</u>.

○ **A.** climate
○ **B.** street
○ **C.** surface
○ **D.** zone

9. The Earth Day booklet listed tips on <u>conserving</u> energy and
lowering costs for heating and air conditioning.

○ **A.** directing
○ **B.** guarding
○ **C.** saving
○ **D.** wasting

10. Water, good soil, and sunlight are <u>critical</u> to a plant's survival.

○ **A.** accepting
○ **B.** nagging
○ **C.** unimportant
○ **D.** vital

Vocabulary
13
Journey to Discovery

Understanding Characters

Identify the choice that best answers the question.

1. Which of these sentences shows that Ruben was excited about the tour?

○ **A.** I looked all over the car for it.

○ **B.** Wow, this is going to be great!

○ **C.** Rosa, your pictures always turn out!

○ **D.** Aren't there 120 steps on the path down?

2. How could you tell that Ranger Jenkins knows a lot about Mesa Verde?

○ **A.** She wrote a book about the park.

○ **B.** She had lived there her whole life.

○ **C.** She answered the children's questions.

○ **D.** She was the person who designed and built the cities.

3. Based on information in this play, which words of advice would Rosa give Ruben?

○ **A.** Never talk to strangers.

○ **B.** Never run with scissors.

○ **C.** Be sure to keep your shoelaces tied.

○ **D.** Pay attention to where you leave things.

4. Which clue helped you know that Ruben was a curious person?

○ **A.** He argued with his sister.

○ **B.** He had visited Mesa Verde many times.

○ **C.** He wanted to know what happened to all of the Ancestral Puebloans.

○ **D.** He used a pen with a digital thermometer so he could tell the temperature.

5. How did the family **most likely** feel when they could not find Rosa?

   ○ **A.** astounded

   ○ **B.** confident

   ○ **C.** embarrassed

   ○ **D.** worried

Mark Student Reading Level:

_____ Independent _____ Instructional _____ Listening

Comprehension
15
Journey to Discovery

Suffixes

Identify the correctly spelled choice that best completes the statement.

1. Lucy's _____ was felt by all of us here.
   - ○ **A.** absence
   - ○ **B.** absentce
   - ○ **C.** absentness
   - ○ **D.** absents

2. There was no _____ at the hotel by the time we got there.
   - ○ **A.** vacancy
   - ○ **B.** vacantcy
   - ○ **C.** vacantness
   - ○ **D.** vancance

3. The _____ of the situation was clear!
   - ○ **A.** urgance
   - ○ **B.** urgancy
   - ○ **C.** urganse
   - ○ **D.** urgency

4. Warren had to measure the _____ of the radio waves.
   - ○ **A.** frequance
   - ○ **B.** frequencie
   - ○ **C.** frequency
   - ○ **D.** frequentness

5. The dancer's _____ seemed to light up the room.
   - ○ **A.** radiance
   - ○ **B.** radianse
   - ○ **C.** radience
   - ○ **D.** radiense

GO ON ➤

Name _____ Date _____

6. I did everything I could to make Grandma
_____.

- A. in comfort
- B. at comfort
- C. comforting
- D. comfortable

7. The police found _____ of the crime.

- A. evidance
- B. evidence
- C. evidency
- D. evidents

8. The program has just begun, so it is in its
_____.

- A. infancy
- B. infansy
- C. infantedness
- D. infantness

9. We went to court and appeared before the _____
Judge Cook.

- A. Honerable
- B. Honereble
- C. Honorable
- D. Honorble

10. The _____ between our homes is six miles.

- A. disance
- B. distance
- C. distence
- D. distince

Assessment Tip: Total 10 points

STOP

Titles and Abbreviations

Identify the choice that best completes the statement.

1. The teacher said, "My name is _____."

   ○ **A.** Ms. Alice N Hawes
   ○ **B.** Ms Alice n Hawes
   ○ **C.** Ms. Alice N. Hawes
   ○ **D.** Ms Alice N. Hawes

2. Mrs. Murray's address is _____.

   ○ **A.** 16 Pumpkin st., Charlton MA
   ○ **B.** 16 Pumpkin ST. Charlton, MA
   ○ **C.** 16 Pumpkin St, Charlton, Ma.
   ○ **D.** 16 Pumpkin St., Charlton, MA

3. My dad's full name is _____.

   ○ **A.** Robert P Altman, Jr.
   ○ **B.** Robert P. Altman, Jnr.
   ○ **C.** Robert P Altman Junior
   ○ **D.** Robert P. Altman, Jr.

4. Because she is a Doctor of Medicine, _____ signs MD after her name.

   ○ **A.** Dr. Wang
   ○ **B.** Doc. Wang
   ○ **C.** Dct. Wang
   ○ **D.** Dr Wang

GO ON ➡

Name _____ Date _____

Language Arts Titles and
Abbreviations

5. For more information about the product, write

to _____ at their Seattle office.

○ **A.** Jones-Wilson Incorp.

○ **B.** Jones-Wilson, Inc.

○ **C.** Jones-Wilson, Incr.

○ **D.** Jones-WIlson, Ink.

6. The short story, _____, is exciting and interesting.

○ **A.** "The tidy Drawer"

○ **B.** *The Tidy Drawer*"

○ **C.** *The Tidy Drawer*

○ **D.** "The Tidy Drawer"

7. I just finished reading a book called _____.

○ **A.** "The beach in Winter"

○ **B.** "The Beach in Winter"

○ **C.** *The Beach in Winter*

○ **D.** "*The Beach in Winter*"

8. We never sing _____ anymore.

○ **A.** three blind mice

○ **B.** "Three Blind Mice"

○ **C.** *Three Blind Mice*

○ **D.** "three blind mice"

9. I saw a movie called _____ yesterday.

○ **A.** "On the Run"

○ **B.** "on the run"

○ **C.** *On the Run*

○ **D.** "*On The Run*"

GO ON ➡

10. The story, _____, is both a book and a movie.

○ **A.** "Pinocchio"

○ **B.** *Pinocchio*

○ **C.** "pinnochio"

○ **D.** *pinocchio*

Name _____ Date _____

TEST RECORD FORM	Possible Score	Criterion Score	Student Score
A: **Vocabulary** Shades of Meaning	10	8	
B: **Comprehension** Fact and Opinion	5	4	
C: **Phonics** Greek Word Roots	10	8	
D: **Language Arts** Commas in Sentences	10	8	
TOTAL	35	28	
Total Student Score x 2.85 =			%

GO ON →

Shades of Meaning

Complete the sentence with the word that has a negative connotation.

1. We worked all day under the _____ sun.
   - ○ **A.** bright
   - ○ **B.** glowing
   - ○ **C.** scorching
   - ○ **D.** shining

2. Peter and Fox had a nasty _____ that had them not speaking for a week.
   - ○ **A.** conflict
   - ○ **B.** disagreement
   - ○ **C.** fight
   - ○ **D.** misunderstanding

3. I knew that Thadeus had an evil _____ up his sleeve.
   - ○ **A.** plan
   - ○ **B.** plot
   - ○ **C.** proposal
   - ○ **D.** trick

Complete the sentence with the word that has a positive connotation.

4. A _____ breeze blew through the town.
   - ○ **A.** chilly
   - ○ **B.** cool
   - ○ **C.** frigid
   - ○ **D.** wintry

GO ON

Vocabulary
22
Journey to Discovery

5. The ice cream was _____ on a warm day.

○ **A.** frigid

○ **B.** icy

○ **C.** piercing

○ **D.** refreshing

Read each sentence. Then find the meaning of the underlined word.

6. The police officer <u>surveyed</u> the scene of the crime.

○ **A.** inspected

○ **B.** measured

○ **C.** planned

○ **D.** tested

7. Rubin made a list of <u>advantages</u> and disadvantages of having a pet.

○ **A.** benefits

○ **B.** conveniences

○ **C.** profits

○ **D.** weaknesses

8. Tales of the old magician's tricks are <u>legendary</u>.

○ **A.** famous

○ **B.** historical

○ **C.** unknown

○ **D.** wicked

9. Cassey tried to <u>persuade</u> Mac to join the chess club.

○ **A.** talk into

○ **B.** work over

○ **C.** wear down

○ **D.** warn against

Vocabulary Shades of Meaning

10. It took some time before electricity was available

in <u>rural</u> areas.

○ **A.** city

○ **B.** country

○ **C.** peaceful

○ **D.** quiet

Fact and Opinion

Identify the choice that best completes the statement or answers the question.

1. Which part of the following quotation is **fact**?

   The Ice Age occurred between 1.6 million and 10,000 years ago. In other words, that tooth was old!

   ○ **A.** all of it

   ○ **B.** none of it

   ○ **C.** *between 1.6 million and 10,000 years*

   ○ **D.** *In other words*

2. Which part of the following quotation is an **opinion**?

   They used their long curving tusks, scientists believe, to shovel snow off the ground to reach buried plants.

   ○ **A.** all of it

   ○ **B.** none of it

   ○ **C.** scientists believe

   ○ **D.** to reach buried plants

3. Which word in the following statement signals that it is an **opinion**?

   Scientists believe they died out due mainly to climate change, disease, and being hunted by early peoples.

   ○ **A.** believe

   ○ **B.** due

   ○ **C.** early

   ○ **D.** mainly

4. On page 41, the author wrote

   ○ **A.** facts only.

   ○ **B.** opinions only.

   ○ **C.** a mixture of facts and opinions.

   ○ **D.** only facts about Mary and her father.

5. To learn facts about the *plesiosaurus*, a reader could do any of the following **except**

○ **A.** talk to an expert.

○ **B.** study the selection.

○ **C.** look in an encyclopedia.

○ **D.** look at reliable sites on the Internet.

Mark Student Reading Level:

_____ Independent _____ Instructional _____ Listening

Greek Word Roots

Choose the word that does not share a root with the others.

1. ○ **A.** phonetic
   ○ **B.** photocopy
   ○ **C.** photograph
   ○ **D.** telephoto

2. ○ **A.** telecommute
   ○ **B.** telepathy
   ○ **C.** telephone
   ○ **D.** telltale

3. ○ **A.** autobiography
   ○ **B.** automobile
   ○ **C.** biography
   ○ **D.** biology

4. ○ **A.** Bible
   ○ **B.** bibliography
   ○ **C.** bibliophile
   ○ **D.** book

5. ○ **A.** megaphone
   ○ **B.** megapod
   ○ **C.** telephone
   ○ **D.** xylophone

6. ○ **A.** autobiography
   ○ **B.** biography
   ○ **C.** photography
   ○ **D.** psychology

GO ON ➤

Phonics Greek Word Roots

7. ○ **A.** lag
   ○ **B.** logic
   ○ **C.** logical
   ○ **D.** logo

8. ○ **A.** declare
   ○ **B.** decade
   ○ **C.** decimal
   ○ **D.** decimal system

9. ○ **A.** home
   ○ **B.** homogeneous
   ○ **C.** homograph
   ○ **D.** homophone

10. ○ **A.** mice
    ○ **B.** microphone
    ○ **C.** microscope
    ○ **D.** microwave

STOP

Commas in Sentences

Identify the correctly written sentence.

1. ○ **A.** Jason, what movie, are your parents taking you to see?

   ○ **B.** Jason, what movie are your parents taking you to see?

   ○ **C.** Jason what movie, are your parents taking you to see?

   ○ **D.** Jason, what movie, are your parents, taking you to see?

2. ○ **A.** Well, I'm not sure of the title.
   ○ **B.** Well I'm not, sure of the title.
   ○ **C.** Well I'm not sure of the title.
   ○ **D.** Well I'm not sure, of the title.

3. ○ **A.** No, Lucas you cannot come with us.
   ○ **B.** No Lucas, you cannot come with us.
   ○ **C.** No Lucas you cannot come with us.
   ○ **D.** No, Lucas, you cannot come with us.

4. ○ **A.** Yes, it's an old black and white movie.
   ○ **B.** Yes it's an old black, and white, movie.
   ○ **C.** Yes it's an old, black, and white movie.
   ○ **D.** Yes it's an old black and white, movie.

5. ○ **A.** Olivia have you seen it, yet?
   ○ **B.** Olivia have you seen it yet?
   ○ **C.** Olivia, have you seen it yet?
   ○ **D.** Olivia have you, seen it, yet?

GO ON ➡

6. ○ **A.** Early in the morning, the family began, to prepare for their trip.

   ○ **B.** Early in the morning the family began to prepare for, their trip.

   ○ **C.** Early in the morning the family began to prepare, for their trip.

   ○ **D.** Early in the morning, the family began to prepare for their trip.

7. ○ **A.** Right before they left Mom put the sandwiches, in the trunk.

   ○ **B.** Right before they left, Mom put the sandwiches in the trunk.

   ○ **C.** Right, before they left Mom put the sandwiches in the trunk.

   ○ **D.** Right, before they left, Mom put the sandwiches in the trunk.

8. ○ **A.** Gloria, who was folding the towels couldn't wait to leave.

   ○ **B.** Gloria, who was folding the towels, couldn't wait to leave.

   ○ **C.** Gloria who was folding the towels, couldn't wait to leave.

   ○ **D.** Gloria, who was folding the towels couldn't, wait to leave.

9. ○ **A.** Zach, a first time diver got his gear ready.

   ○ **B.** Zach a first time diver, got his gear ready.

   ○ **C.** Zach, a first time diver, got his gear ready.

   ○ **D.** Zach, a first time diver got his gear, ready.

10. ○ **A.** Hortense, Mom's friend came with us too.

    ○ **B.** Hortense, Mom's friend came with us, too.

    ○ **C.** Hortense Mom's friend, came with us too.

    ○ **D.** Hortense, Mom's friend, came with us too.

Name _____ Date _____

TEST RECORD FORM	Possible Score	Criterion Score	Student Score
A: Vocabulary Greek and Latin Roots	10	8	
B: Comprehension Conclusions and Generalizations	5	4	
C: Phonics Latin Word Roots	10	8	
D: Language Arts Commas in Sentences	10	8	
TOTAL	35	28	
Total Student Score x 2.85 =			%

GO ON

Greek and Latin Roots

Identify the choice that best defines the underlined word.

1. I wish Jack would stop <u>interrupting</u> the conversation.
   - ○ **A.** changing
   - ○ **B.** coming in during
   - ○ **C.** making a lot of noise during
   - ○ **D.** breaking into with comments

2. I would like a <u>section</u> of that orange.
   - ○ **A.** taste
   - ○ **B.** smell
   - ○ **C.** cut piece
   - ○ **D.** uncut piece

3. Can you <u>transport</u> my luggage for me?
   - ○ **A.** pack
   - ○ **B.** bring
   - ○ **C.** check in at the airport
   - ○ **D.** carry from one place to another

4. The radio is <u>portable</u>.
   - ○ **A.** light
   - ○ **B.** heavy
   - ○ **C.** able to be carried
   - ○ **D.** not able to be carried

5. The volcano has <u>erupted</u> many times.
   - ○ **A.** changed
   - ○ **B.** burst forth
   - ○ **C.** been seen
   - ○ **D.** been studied

GO ON

6. Jim was <u>incredibly</u> brave when he rescued the child from the burning house.

   - ○ **A.** barely
   - ○ **B.** hardly
   - ○ **C.** slightly
   - ○ **D.** tremendously

7. Laura will reach her <u>destination</u> at 5:45 P.M.

   - ○ **A.** the beginning of a journey
   - ○ **B.** a purpose for making a journey
   - ○ **C.** a stop in the middle of a journey
   - ○ **D.** a place where someone is going

8. By studying the chimpanzees, the biologists will gain <u>insights</u> into their behavior patterns.

   - ○ **A.** ignorance
   - ○ **B.** mistakes
   - ○ **C.** understanding
   - ○ **D.** wisdom

9. Barney found an <u>effective</u> way to get his classmates to recycle paper.

   - ○ **A.** without any result
   - ○ **B.** having the wrong result
   - ○ **C.** having the desired result
   - ○ **D.** without the desired result

10. After Anna returned from Mexico, her little brother <u>plagued</u> her with questions about her trip.

   - ○ **A.** comforted
   - ○ **B.** pestered
   - ○ **C.** relieved
   - ○ **D.** teased

Name _____ Date _____

Conclusions and Generalizations

**Identify the choice that best completes the statement
or answers the question.**

1. From information in the story, you could tell that

   ○ **A.** it was rainy during Blake's vacation.
   ○ **B.** Maria and Blake went to school together.
   ○ **C.** Grandpa had been to the cabins in the past.
   ○ **D.** Nicholas and Todd wanted to learn how to play soccer.

2. At the beginning of the story, how did Blake feel about seeing the deer?

   ○ **A.** anxious
   ○ **B.** furious
   ○ **C.** scared
   ○ **D.** timid

3. Which of these would be the most helpful to a person who wanted to be a good detective?

   ○ **A.** working where the weather is very cold
   ○ **B.** having money to buy expensive equipment
   ○ **C.** being able to find clues and figure out what they mean
   ○ **D.** knowing how to grow and harvest different kinds of crops

4. To find out where the deer had been, the children looked for

   ○ **A.** hair on branches.
   ○ **B.** tracks on the ground.
   ○ **C.** apples with bite marks.
   ○ **D.** antlers that were broken.

GO ON

5. Maria is good at

- ○ **A.** observing because she noticed the sweatshirt.
- ○ **B.** playing soccer because she scored all the points.
- ○ **C.** cooking because she makes meals for her family.
- ○ **D.** learning new things because she reads a lot of books.

Comprehension Conclusions and Generalizations

Mark Student Reading Level:

_____ Independent _____ Instructional _____ Listening

Latin Word Parts

Identify the choice that does not have the same Latin word part as the others.

1. ○ **A.** exchange
   ○ **B.** export
   ○ **C.** portal
   ○ **D.** report

2. ○ **A.** special
   ○ **B.** spectacles
   ○ **C.** spectator
   ○ **D.** speculate

3. ○ **A.** corrupt
   ○ **B.** disrupt
   ○ **C.** disturb
   ○ **D.** erupt

4. ○ **A.** portable
   ○ **B.** transfer
   ○ **C.** transmit
   ○ **D.** transport

5. ○ **A.** construct
   ○ **B.** construction
   ○ **C.** structure
   ○ **D.** traction

6. ○ **A.** dictate
   ○ **B.** dictionary
   ○ **C.** product
   ○ **D.** verdict

GO ON →

7. ○ **A.** contradict
   ○ **B.** diction
   ○ **C.** verdict
   ○ **D.** vermin

8. ○ **A.** retort
   ○ **B.** retrofit
   ○ **C.** retrograde
   ○ **D.** retrospect

9. ○ **A.** correct
   ○ **B.** corrupt
   ○ **C.** disrupt
   ○ **D.** rupture

10. ○ **A.** respect
    ○ **B.** spectacles
    ○ **C.** speculate
    ○ **D.** speedy

STOP

Assessment Tip: Total 10 points

Commas in Sentences

Identify the correctly written sentence.

1. ○ **A.** Pete, our class president has been absent a lot.
   ○ **B.** Pete our class president, has been absent a lot.
   ○ **C.** Pete, our class president, has been absent a lot.
   ○ **D.** Pete, our class president has been, absent a lot.

2. ○ **A.** Leila, the most talented writer in our class has written him a letter.
   ○ **B.** Leila the most talented writer in our class, has written him a letter.
   ○ **C.** Leila the most talented writer in our class has written him a letter.
   ○ **D.** Leila, the most talented writer in our class, has written him a letter.

3. ○ **A.** Darcy, the white dog with the black spots, is barking.
   ○ **B.** Darcy, the white dog, with the black spots, is barking.
   ○ **C.** Darcy, the white, dog with the black, spots is barking.
   ○ **D.** Darcy the white dog, with the black spots, is barking.

4. ○ **A.** Celia Rachel, and I live in Austin, Texas.
   ○ **B.** Celia, Rachel and I live in Austin Texas.
   ○ **C.** Celia, Rachel, and I live in Austin, Texas.
   ○ **D.** Celia, Rachel, and I, live in Austin, Texas.

5. ○ **A.** I went to Washington D.C. on December, 11 2005.
   ○ **B.** I went to Washington, D.C. on December 11 2005.
   ○ **C.** I went to Washington, D.C. on December 11, 2005.
   ○ **D.** I went to Washington, D.C. on December, 11, 2005.

GO ON

6. ○ **A.** Polly our parakeet with the yellow tail, is from New Mexico.

   ○ **B.** Polly our parakeet with the yellow tail is from New, Mexico.

   ○ **C.** Polly, our parakeet with the yellow tail, is from New Mexico.

   ○ **D.** Polly, our parakeet with the yellow tail, is from New, Mexico.

7. ○ **A.** Cindy Lisa and Penny, went to, the store.

   ○ **B.** Cindy, Lisa, and Penny went to the store.

   ○ **C.** Cindy, Lisa, and Penny, went to the store.

   ○ **D.** Cindy, Lisa and Penny went, to the store.

8. ○ **A.** I wanted to go home on Thursday, July 15 2007.

   ○ **B.** I wanted to go home on Thursday July, 15 2007.

   ○ **C.** I wanted to go home on Thursday, July 15, 2007.

   ○ **D.** I wanted to go home on, Thursday July 15 2007.

9. ○ **A.** We bought pies cakes, cookies and candies.

   ○ **B.** We bought pies cakes cookies, and candies.

   ○ **C.** We bought pies, cakes cookies and candies.

   ○ **D.** We bought pies, cakes, cookies, and candies.

10. ○ **A.** I am going to Reno, Nevada, on June 16, 2008.

    ○ **B.** I am going to Reno Nevada, on June 16 2008.

    ○ **C.** I am going to Reno Nevada on June 16, 2008.

    ○ **D.** I am going to Reno, Nevada on June 16 2008.

Assessment Tip: Total 10 points

Name _____ Date _____

TEST RECORD FORM	Possible Score	Criterion Score	Student Score
A: **Vocabulary** Word Origins	10	8	
B: **Comprehension** Topic, Main Idea, and Details	5	4	
C: **Phonics** Identifying Syllable Patterns	10	8	
D: **Language Arts** Other Punctuation	10	8	
TOTAL	35	28	
Total Student Score x 2.85 =			%

GO ON

Word Origins

Identify the choice that best answers the question.

Vocabulary Dictionary

absolute *adj.* perfect, complete [from Latin *absolutus*, to loosen from]

alligator *n.* large crocodilian reptile [from Spanish, *el lagarto*, *the lizard*]

cocoa *n.* powder made from cacao seeds [from Spanish, *cacao*, cacao]

domain *n.* land belonging to one person [from Latin, *dominium*, right of ownership]

---

1. On what word or words is the word *alligator* based?

   ○ **A.** the Latin word *absolutus*
   ○ **B.** the Spanish word *lagarto*
   ○ **C.** the Latin words *el lagarto*
   ○ **D.** the Spanish words *el lagarto*

2. From what language did the word *absolute* originate?

   ○ **A.** Latin
   ○ **B.** French
   ○ **C.** Spanish
   ○ **D.** Middle English

3. What is the meaning of *dominium*?

   ○ **A.** home
   ○ **B.** to loosen from
   ○ **C.** right of ownership
   ○ **D.** land belonging to one person

GO ON

4. Which word origin is exactly the same in Spanish and in English?

  ○ **A.** *cacao*
  ○ **B.** cocoa
  ○ **C.** el lagarto
  ○ **D.** dominium

Read each sentence. Then find the meaning of the underlined word.

5. Kira is <u>undoubtedly</u> the best gymnast on the team.

  ○ **A.** full of doubt
  ○ **B.** having doubt
  ○ **C.** without a doubt
  ○ **D.** unable to doubt

6. José <u>reasoned</u> that he could have his cake and eat it, too!

  ○ **A.** studied
  ○ **B.** pondered
  ○ **C.** figured out
  ○ **D.** planned out

7. Route 66 is one of the oldest highways in the U.S., <u>extending</u> from Chicago to Los Angeles.

  ○ **A.** climbing
  ○ **B.** leaving
  ○ **C.** ranging
  ○ **D.** soaring

8. At first, Vera <u>balked</u> at paying so much for the movie ticket, but later, she changed her mind.

  ○ **A.** agreed
  ○ **B.** insisted
  ○ **C.** prevented
  ○ **D.** refused

GO ON →

9. Judy <u>underestimated</u> the value of her grandmother's clock and sold it for a small price.

○ **A.** set low
○ **B.** took away
○ **C.** appreciated
○ **D.** exaggerated

10. The team was <u>optimistic</u> about winning the football game.

○ **A.** hopeful
○ **B.** hopeless
○ **C.** unhappy
○ **D.** unsure

STOP

Topic, Main Idea, and Details

Comprehension Topic,
Main Idea, and Details

Identify the choice that best answers the question.

1. What question does this story answer?

   ○ **A.** What is a maze?

   ○ **B.** Who made the first maze?

   ○ **C.** When were mazes invented?

   ○ **D.** Which maze is the shortest in the world?

2. Which best summarizes what a labyrinth is?

   ○ **A.** Labyrinths have a single path leading from beginning to end.

   ○ **B.** Labyrinths are simple designs built into a floor or other flat surface.

   ○ **C.** Labyrinths, which are simple designs built into a flat surface, have a single path leading from beginning to end.

   ○ **D.** Labyrinths are often confused with mazes, but labyrinths, which are often made from tiles or large stones, sometimes do not have any walls at all.

3. Why do yews make good borders for mazes?

   ○ **A.** They can be grown in any climate.

   ○ **B.** They grow slowly and keep their shape.

   ○ **C.** They can be grown in countries all over the world.

   ○ **D.** They grow quickly and can be molded into different shapes.

4. Which maze winds through an underground cave?

   ○ **A.** Leeds Castle

   ○ **B.** Silver Jubilee

   ○ **C.** Maze of the Minotaur

   ○ **D.** Longleat Hedge Maze

5. What kind of beast was the Minotaur?

○ **A.** a lion

○ **B.** a dinosaur

◉ **C.** part bull and part man

○ **D.** part pig and part cowboy

Mark Student Reading Level:

_____ Independent _____ Instructional _____ Listening

Name _____ Date _____

Identifying Syllable Patterns

Identify the choice that best completes the statement.

1. Will you go with me to see the _____?
   ○ **A.** balet
   ○ **B.** ballat
   ○ **C.** ballet
   ○ **D.** ballot

2. I am going to wear my _____ pants.
   ○ **A.** kakhi
   ○ **B.** kaki
   ○ **C.** khaki
   ○ **D.** khaky

3. It will _____ Juan if you show that photograph.
   ○ **A.** embaras
   ○ **B.** embarrass
   ○ **C.** embarress
   ○ **D.** embarriss

4. The little girl wore a _____ in her hair.
   ○ **A.** barete
   ○ **B.** barette
   ○ **C.** barrete
   ○ **D.** barrette

5. There was a beautiful _____ of flowers waiting for me
   at home.
   ○ **A.** bewquet
   ○ **B.** boquet
   ○ **C.** bouquet
   ○ **D.** bouquyt

6. I would like to see the movie's _____.

   ○ **A.** premeere

   ○ **B.** premeire

   ○ **C.** premere

   ◉ **D.** premiere

7. Lexi wrote an _____ in one hour.

   ○ **A.** eassy

   ◉ **B.** essay

   ○ **C.** essey

   ○ **D.** essy

8. Oskar and his father are going on a _____.

   ◉ **A.** safari

   ○ **B.** saferi

   ○ **C.** seafari

   ○ **D.** sefari

9. What is the _____ of that song?

   ○ **A.** choras

   ◉ **B.** chorus

   ○ **C.** corous

   ○ **D.** korus

10. My pants are made of _____.

   ○ **A.** denam

   ○ **B.** denem

   ◉ **C.** denim

   ○ **D.** denum

STOP

Other Punctuation

Identify the choice that best completes the statement or answers the question.

> Dear Ariel
>
> It is now six forty two in the evening and I am writing to let you know what I need from the grocery store tomorrow. Here is my list
>
> apples
> oranges
> bread the kind that has a thick crust
> eggs
>
> Thank you for getting those things for me.
>
> Sincerely
>
> Tara

1. The time in the letter should be written _____.

- A. 642
- B. 6:42
- C. 6;42
- D. 6, 42

2. After *Sincerely* the letter writer should add _____.

- A. nothing
- B. a colon
- C. a comma
- D. a semicolon

GO ON

3. After the word *list* the letter writer should add _____.

○ **A.** nothing

○ **B.** a colon

○ **C.** a comma

○ **D.** a semicolon

4. After *Ariel* the letter writer should add a _____

○ **A.** colon

○ **B.** comma

○ **C.** semicolon

○ **D.** exclamation mark

5. After the word *bread*, the description of the bread could be punctuated by _____.

○ **A.** using a comma

○ **B.** adding brackets

○ **C.** using a semicolon

○ **D.** adding parentheses

6. Which properly begins a business letter?

○ **A.** Dear Mr. Smith,

○ **B.** Dear Mr. Smith:

○ **C.** Dear Mr. Smith;

○ **D.** Dear Mr, Smith,

Identify the correctly punctuated sentence.

7. ○ **A.** At 400 I will take a nap.

○ **B.** At 4 00 I will take a nap

○ **C.** At 4:00 I will take a nap.

○ **D.** At 4;00 I will take a nap

8. ○ **A.** I have the following requests. turn off the lights; pull down the shades; and hang up the phone.

   ○ **B.** I have the following requests: turn off the lights pull down the shades and hang up the phone.

   ○ **C.** I have the following requests: turn off the lights, pull down the shades, and hang up the phone.

   ○ **D.** I have the following requests; turn off the lights, pull down the shades, and hang up the phone.

9. ○ **A.** Please wash my shirt, the blue one and my pants the green ones.

   ○ **B.** Please wash my shirt (the blue one and my pants the green ones).

   ○ **C.** Please wash my shirt (the blue one) and my pants the green ones.

   ○ **D.** Please wash my shirt (the blue one) and my pants (the green ones).

10. ○ **A.** At 725 let's get in the car and go.

   ○ **B.** At 7,25 let's get in the car and go.

   ○ **C.** At 7:25 let's get in the car and go.

   ○ **D.** At 7;25 let's get in the car and go.

STOP

Alternative Assessments:
Novel Comprehension Tests

Name _____ Date _____

Skunk Scout

Identify the choice that best completes the statement or answers the question.

1. Teddy is upset when his father tells him that he will give Teddy the fish store when he grows up, because

   ○ **A.** Teddy hates fish.
   ○ **B.** Teddy's father's hands always smell.
   ○ **C.** Bobby is the one who deserves the fish store.
   ○ **D.** Teddy is not sure he is ready to decide what his future will be.

2. Why does Teddy play the *only child game?*

   ○ **A.** It is a fun game.
   ○ **B.** to annoy his brother
   ○ **C.** Teddy hates his brother.
   ○ **D.** He has mixed feelings about having a brother.

3. Why did Teddy try to learn about the outdoors from one of Bobby's books?

   ○ **A.** He was curious.
   ○ **B.** to impress Bobby and Uncle Curtis
   ○ **C.** He wanted to prepare himself for camping.
   ○ **D.** to convince his grandmother that camping would be safe

4. On the way to the camping place, why does Uncle Curtis keep losing his way?

   ○ **A.** He gets distracted easily.
   ○ **B.** The boys tell him to go in the wrong direction.
   ○ **C.** He is testing the boys to see if they know their way.
   ○ **D.** He wants the boys to tell Grandmother that they got lost.

Skunk Scout
Comprehension

5. Who was best at finding the way when the group was lost?

  ○ **A.** Bobby
  ○ **B.** Curtis
  ○ **C.** Grandmother
  ○ **D.** Teddy

6. What *big as a mountain* mistake does Teddy make that prevents the group from eating good meals?

  ○ **A.** He brings candy with him.
  ○ **B.** He puts the food in an ice chest with dry ice.
  ○ **C.** He brings marshmallows that attract a raccoon.
  ○ **D.** He forgets the ice chest at home with all of the food in it.

7. What does Teddy discover about Uncle Curtis on the camping trip that changes how Teddy feels about him?

  ○ **A.** Uncle Curtis is a lot like Teddy.
  ○ **B.** Uncle Curtis is his father's brother.
  ○ **C.** Uncle Curtis wants to go home too.
  ○ **D.** Uncle Curtis likes Teddy better than he likes Bobby.

8. Teddy begins to enjoy the hike when he

  ○ **A.** sees a bear.
  ○ **B.** finds the way back.
  ○ **C.** notices the sights and smells of nature.
  ○ **D.** has a long talk with Uncle Curtis about not wanting to own a fish store.

9. The most fascinating thing that Teddy saw on the trip was the

  ○ **A.** skunk.
  ○ **B.** raccoon.
  ○ **C.** television antennas.
  ○ **D.** courtship of the snakes.

GO ON

10. Where did Lawrence Yep get his ideas for the camping adventures in *Skunk Scout?*

○ **A.** *Skunk Scout* is an autobiography.

○ **B.** The stories in *Skunk Scout* are from Yep's imagination.

○ **C.** *Skunk Scout* is based only on things that actually happened to Yep.

○ **D.** *Skunk Scout* is based on things that happened to Yep and to people he knows.

STOP

Frindle

Identify the choice that best completes the statement or answers the question.

1. The main purpose of the illustration on page 30 is to show that
   - ○ **A.** dogs are important in this story.
   - ○ **B.** dogs come in many varieties.
   - ○ **C.** Mrs. Granger knows a lot about dogs.
   - ○ **D.** there are many different words for "dog."

2. Which of the following statements best defines Nick's character?
   - ○ **A.** Nick is a troublemaker.
   - ○ **B.** Nick is determined.
   - ○ **C.** Nick is bossy.
   - ○ **D.** Nick is stubborn.

3. What event leads Nick to invent the word *frindle*?
   - ○ **A.** He returns Janet's gold pen.
   - ○ **B.** He buys a pen at a store.
   - ○ **C.** He remembers saying *frindle* as a child.
   - ○ **D.** He finds a pen on the street.

4. The oath Nick's classmates take to say *frindle* supports which main idea?
   - ○ **A.** It's important to keep a promise.
   - ○ **B.** Students should decide what they learn.
   - ○ **C.** Words will spread if enough people use them.
   - ○ **D.** Nick makes the rules.

5. Why does Mrs. Granger punish students for saying *frindle*?
   - ○ **A.** She thinks students are being disrespectful.
   - ○ **B.** She thinks students should follow the rules.
   - ○ **C.** She thinks opposing the word will stop its use.
   - ○ **D.** She thinks opposing the word will help spread its use.

6. Which of the following statements is a fact?
   - ○ **A.** "The dictionary is the finest tool ever made for educating young minds."
   - ○ **B.** "All the words in the dictionary were made up by people."
   - ○ **C.** "She's really a very fine teacher."
   - ○ **D.** "As the boy's guardian, you need to do the right thing about all this."

7. What conclusion can you draw about Mrs. Granger from the letter she has Nick sign?
   - ○ **A.** She likes to keep records of everything.
   - ○ **B.** She is mysterious.
   - ○ **C.** She wants Nick to succeed with his word.
   - ○ **D.** She wants Nick to fail with his word.

8. What is the main idea supported by the news broadcast about *frindle*?
   - ○ **A.** The news media spreads ideas to lots of people.
   - ○ **B.** The news media causes people to argue.
   - ○ **C.** The news media makes Nick famous.
   - ○ **D.** TV is more important than newspapers.

GO ON

9. Which conclusion is supported by the illustration on page 103?

- ○ **A.** Nick hates to study.
- ○ **B.** Nick still likes baseball.
- ○ **C.** Nick prefers a pen to a computer.
- ○ **D.** Nick doesn't remember Mrs. Granger.

10. Why does Nick "win" in the end?

- ○ **A.** because he becomes rich
- ○ **B.** because he does well in college
- ○ **C.** because *frindle* is listed in the dictionary
- ○ **D.** because Mrs. Granger gives up

Mysteries of the Mummy Kids

Identify the choice that best completes the statement or answers the question.

1. What is the author's purpose in writing *Mysteries of the Mummy Kids?*

   ○ **A.** to entertain
   ○ **B.** to inform readers about King Tut
   ○ **C.** to inform readers about mummies
   ○ **D.** to persuade readers to study historical cultures

2. What causes a body to become a mummy?

   ○ **A.** water in the body
   ○ **B.** lack of water in the body
   ○ **C.** It's a mystery—nobody knows.
   ○ **D.** the wrapping of the body in fabric

3. In general, how do experts explain why the Incas sacrificed children?

   ○ **A.** The deaths resulted from wars.
   ○ **B.** The experts have no explanation.
   ○ **C.** They were thanking the gods for providing food and shelter.
   ○ **D.** They were asking the gods to provide good weather and help them win wars.

4. What caused the El Plomo boy's body to mummify?

   ○ **A.** a chemical process
   ○ **B.** the frigid temperatures of the Andes
   ○ **C.** a special ceremony in honor of the gods
   ○ **D.** the work of an anthropologist named D. Johan Reinhard

GO ON

5. Which is a summary of one difference between the Incas' Andean mummies and the Chinchorros' mummies?

   ○ **A.** The Incas peeled the skin off the bodies and the Chinchorros did not.

   ○ **B.** The Incas buried their dead in graveyards and the Chinchorros did not.

   ○ **C.** The Incas' Andean mummies died of natural causes and the Chinchorros' were killed.

   ○ **D.** The Incas' Andean mummies were purposely killed and the Chinchorros' died of natural causes.

6. Civilization's oldest mummies were found in

   ○ **A.** Chile

   ○ **B.** Egypt

   ○ **C.** Greenland

   ○ **D.** Sicily

7. King Tut's cause of death was never determined because

   ○ **A.** autopsy is against the religion of the Egyptians.

   ○ **B.** his body was not handled with care when discovered.

   ○ **C.** his body was not handled with care when mummified.

   ○ **D.** seventy-five years went by between discovering the body and trying to date his death.

8. How do experts know that Tut was a king?

   ○ **A.** oral history

   ○ **B.** written history

   ○ **C.** He was buried with the objects of a king.

   ○ **D.** The location of his tomb was where a king's tomb would be.

GO ON

9. What preserved the mummies of northwestern Europe's bog people?

○ **A.** peat
○ **B.** water
○ **C.** chemicals
○ **D.** freezing temperatures

10. What does the author suggest about the future of mummification?

○ **A.** It has no future.
○ **B.** It will definitely be common practice.
○ **C.** It is possible that it will be common practice.
○ **D.** It is illegal and could never happen in the future.

Name _____ Date _____

Bill Pickett: Rodeo King

The most famous African American cowboy of his time, Bill | 10
Pickett entertained thousands of people around the world, from | 19
ordinary folks to royalty. | 23

Bill Pickett was born on December 5, 1870, in Travis County, | 34
Texas. His father, Thomas Jefferson Pickett, had been a slave | 44
until slavery ended in the United States in 1865. Both Thomas | 55
and his wife, Mary, had black, white, and Native American | 65
ancestors. | 66

Pickett, the oldest of thirteen children, grew up near Austin. | 76
He was a bright student at the one-room school he attended. He | 88
learned to read and write. But he only went to school through | 100
the fifth grade. Since his family was very poor, Pickett had to go | 113
to work while still a boy to help earn money. | 123

Growing up in Texas, Pickett eagerly watched cowboys at | 132
work. He saw them drive herds of longhorn cattle along the | 143
dusty trail from Austin to Kansas stockyards. Spellbound, he | 152
listened to his older cousins' stories about their adventures on | 162
cattle drives. At that time, cattle didn't graze within one fenced- | 173
in ranch area. | 175

The country had grown so large that when it was time to | 187
take them to the cattle market, the cows had to be rounded | 199
up from the West and herded to a stockyard in the East or to | 213
a railway that could take them there. The cattle drive usually | 224
lasted a month and covered 2,000 miles. The cowboys had to | 235
look out for Indians and rustlers, and find pastures along the way. | 247

When Pickett left school, he decided to become a ranch | 257
hand. He learned how to ride horses and throw a lasso. He even | 270
learned how to tame a wild mustang. Strong and agile, he could | 282
think quickly and move fast. He knew a lot about horses and | 294
could predict how they would behave. | 300

One day young Bill saw a rancher using some dogs to round | 312
up some stray cattle. The dogs were part bulldog, a breed that is | 325
known for biting and hanging on no matter what. The dogs used | 337
a special technique to subdue the cows. When they caught | 347

Bill Pickett: Rodeo King (continued)

up with one, they leapt up and grabbed onto its upper lip with	360
their teeth. Since this lip is very sensitive, the cow came to a	373
shuddering stop and didn't move. The rancher could then take	383
his time roping it. This method of catching cattle was called	394
bulldogging.	395
While he was a ranch hand, Pickett developed all the skills	406
a cowboy needed. He also experimented with new ways to	416
handle livestock. One day, Pickett helped a group of cowboys	426
brand some ornery calves. He told them he could quiet any calf.	438
The cowboys laughed at him but agreed to let him try. He used	451
the "bite-'em style" he learned from the rancher's dogs. To the	462
cowboys' amazement, Pickett managed to quiet the frisky calves.	471
He later used this technique when he performed in rodeos and	482
shows.	483
In the late 1880's, Pickett moved to Taylor, Texas. A local	494
rancher hired him to feed and work his cattle. Now and for	506
nearly the rest of his life, Pickett was officially a cowboy. He	518
would have plenty of chances to perfect his bulldogging	527
technique.	528

Words in 3 mins.		_____	Retelling _____	Expression _____	
Minus errors	−	_____	(See Weekly Tests rubrics)	(See Weekly Tests rubrics)	
Total correct	=	_____	☐ Excellent	☐ Expected progress	
Divide (3 mins.)	÷	3	☐ Good	☐ Below expected	
Words Correct Per Minute	=	_____	☐ Needs Improvement	☐ Seriously below expected	

Bill Pickett: Rodeo King

The most famous African American cowboy of his time, Bill Pickett entertained thousands of people around the world, from ordinary folks to royalty.

Bill Pickett was born on December 5, 1870, in Travis County, Texas. His father, Thomas Jefferson Pickett, had been a slave until slavery ended in the United States in 1865. Both Thomas and his wife, Mary, had black, white, and Native American ancestors.

Pickett, the oldest of thirteen children, grew up near Austin. He was a bright student at the one-room school he attended. He learned to read and write. But he only went to school through the fifth grade. Since his family was very poor, Pickett had to go to work while still a boy to help earn money.

Growing up in Texas, Pickett eagerly watched cowboys at work. He saw them drive herds of longhorn cattle along the dusty trail from Austin to Kansas stockyards. Spellbound, he listened to his older cousins' stories about their adventures on cattle drives. At that time, cattle didn't graze within one fenced-in ranch area.

The country had grown so large that when it was time to take them to the cattle market, the cows had to be rounded up from the West and herded to a stockyard in the East or to a railway that could take them there. The cattle drive usually lasted a month and covered 2,000 miles. The cowboys had to look out for Indians and rustlers, and find pastures along the way.

When Pickett left school, he decided to become a ranch hand. He learned how to ride horses and throw a lasso. He even learned how to tame a wild mustang. Strong and agile, he could think quickly and move fast. He knew a lot about horses and could predict how they would behave.

One day young Bill saw a rancher using some dogs to round up some stray cattle. The dogs were part bulldog, a breed that is known for biting and hanging on no matter what. The dogs used a special technique to subdue the cows. When they caught

Bill Pickett: Rodeo King (continued)

up with one, they leapt up and grabbed onto its upper lip with their teeth. Since this lip is very sensitive, the cow came to a shuddering stop and didn't move. The rancher could then take his time roping it. This method of catching cattle was called bulldogging.

While he was a ranch hand, Pickett developed all the skills a cowboy needed. He also experimented with new ways to handle livestock. One day, Pickett helped a group of cowboys brand some ornery calves. He told them he could quiet any calf. The cowboys laughed at him but agreed to let him try. He used the "bite-'em style" he learned from the rancher's dogs. To the cowboys' amazement, Pickett managed to quiet the frisky calves. He later used this technique when he performed in rodeos and shows.

In the late 1880's, Pickett moved to Taylor, Texas. A local rancher hired him to feed and work his cattle. Now and for nearly the rest of his life, Pickett was officially a cowboy. He would have plenty of chances to perfect his bulldogging technique.

Name _____ Date _____

Note: Occasionally a student may finish a passage before the end of three minutes. If the scores for Decoding Accuracy and Comprehension are also above the on-level benchmarks, assume that the student is reading beyond the grade level tested and reassess with a higher passage.

Phrasing and Expression

- Refer to the Fluency: Phrasing and Expression Rubric below. In general, students who score a 3 or 4 are judged to have adequate phrasing and expression. Those scoring 1 or 2 are exhibiting some difficulty. Note that students do not have to read flawlessly to score a 4.

- Enter the score on the Recording Form. You will probably find it easier to get an accurate score if you enter it immediately after the student's oral reading or after listening to the tape recording.

Phrasing and Expression Rubric

Score	Description
4	Reads primarily in larger, meaningful phrases. Although the student may make some errors or repetitions, these do not appear to detract from the overall structure of the story. Most of the story is read with expressive interpretation, guided by meaning and punctuation.
3	Reads primarily in three- or four-word phrases, although there are some word-by-word slowdowns. However, the majority of phrasing seems appropriate and preserves the author's meaning. Some expressive interpretation is evident.
2	Reads primarily in two-word phrases with some three- and four-word groupings. Some word-by-word reading may be present. Word groupings may seem awkward and unrelated to meaning. Little expressive interpretation is evident.
1	Reads primarily word-by-word. Two- or three-word phrases may occur occasionally, but these are infrequent and/or they do not preserve meaning. No expression is evident.

Name _____ Date _____

Retelling

- Consult your notes from the retelling.
- Use the rubric below to evaluate it.

Comprehension: Retelling Rubric

Score	Description
4	Includes the main idea or problem, all significant events or information, many supporting details; retelling is organized in proper sequence and is coherent.
3	Includes the main idea or problem, most significant events, some details; may include some minor misinformation; retelling is generally organized and sequenced.
2	Has some information from the passage but misses the main idea or problem; may have a few key events, information, or details but not integrated into the larger story; little organization or sequence.
1	Little or no content is included in the retelling; may include some points from the passage, mostly details, but misses the main idea or problem and significant ideas; retelling is unfocused, sketchy; misinformation or little information.